**BEGINNING
KUNG-FU**

BEGINNING
KUNG-FU

BY KAM YUEN

©Ohara Publications, Incorporated 1975
All rights reserved
Printed in the United States of America
Library of Congress Catalog Card Number: 75-21721

Seventeenth Printing 1984
ISBN-0-89750-042-3

GRAPHIC DESIGN BY DAVID PAUL KAPLAN

OHARA 🄾 PUBLICATIONS, INCORPORATED

BURBANK, CALIFORNIA

DEDICATION

Janet Watson, John Robinson and David Carradine

ABOUT THE AUTHOR

Kam Yuen was born in Hong Kong and has studied the Northern System of kung-fu in the Orient and the Chinese communities of San Francisco and New York. He is presently the national director of the Tai Mantis Kung-Fu Association and has taught his art at the University of Southern California, at California State in Los Angeles and at the University of Los Angeles. Besides being called upon to demonstrate at various martial arts tournaments, Yuen was also the technical and kung-fu advisor for ABC's weekly "Kung Fu" series. There, he worked as David Carradine's double for the difficult fight scenes and acted as one of the masters in the Shaolin Temple.

Kam Yuen's list of abilities include a proficiency in the Northern Shaolin System, Eighteen Law-Horn Forms, Seven Star Praying Mantis, Tai Chi Praying Mantis, Tai Chi Chuan and the use of numerous weapons of the Northern Shaolin System.

INTRODUCTION

Throughout 1974, KARATE ILLUSTRATED carried a monthly series of beginning kung-fu in lesson form. The course was designed to supplement regular training in the kwoon and to increase the efficiency of the student practicing his lessons away from the kwoon.

Because of favorable reader response and the difficulty of obtaining a complete set of all the lessons in back issues, they are presented here in book form with a few additions.

Bear in mind that the course is in no way to be regarded as a substitute for a course of instruction under a skilled teacher in a kwoon.

To make satisfactory progress, perform the lessons at least three times a week. The use of a full-length mirror affords the best comparison of your progress and proficiency with the ideal form as illustrated in the photos. Spend two hours in each practice session.

In the illustrated material, John Robinson and Janet Watson demonstrate the exercises of the Tai Mantis Kung-Fu style. Please note, as the lessons progress, combinations utilizing more sophisticated techniques are introduced to increase the students' concepts of power, timing, balance, speed and stamina as applied to the Northern Shaolin Monastery System.

Avoid strain.

SELECTING THE KWOON

Pay a visit to each kwoon available in your area. Observe classes in session. Compare the different styles. Choose the one that most appeals to your needs. Quality of instruction counts. Observe the class discipline and the respect each student pays the instructor. Question the finance, traveling time and distance, but do not let these factors determine your choice of instructor or kwoon. It is what happens at the lesson that counts.

Observe lessons more than once. You will better be able to evaluate the effectiveness and emphasis of instruction and the characteristics of style. Does the course emphasize total development of the participant? Are speed, flexibility, strength, coordination, alertness and flowing movements fit into a pattern of training that suits the individual's needs? Do they assure his progress?

Is there a balance of body conditioning as well as instruction on kung-fu techniques? Form and free sparring should be part of each lesson.

Instruction should stress flexibility and fluidity of movement. It should not be a study of street fighting techniques, nor should it be a study of techniques executed from a stationary position with little movement or footwork.

Examine the instructor's background, the legitimacy of his style, and the affiliation of his organization. Avoid accepting as valid any vague claims such as high rank with such grand titles as professor, doctor, grand master, founder and sole instructor of a new system and style. Shun the member of an underground secret society or the graduate of an untraceable monastery.

Avoid commitment to a kwoon professing to teach all styles as well as numerous animal styles of kung-fu. One animal form does not constitute a kung-fu style. Numerous hand and weapons forms do.

Avoid casting your lot with instructors whose only claim is having learned exclusively from ancestors who are unknown in the martial arts. Regard as hearsay accounts you may be given of an instructor's feats and abilities. Check it out. Be skeptical of overweight and out of condition instructors whose obesity indicates lack of discipline, laziness, and general disregard for the art. These may be the ones who claim to teach internal development, quick results, and scientific improvements, yet neglect body conditioning.

There is no set length of time required for one to become proficient in kung-fu. Progress varies with each individual's natural abilities and his determination and dedication to proficiency. Consistent training spells the difference between success and failure. Fast learners do not always go the furthest. A slow starter often accepts the challenge of study, and by persevering becomes proficient. Size, sex, and age are not limiting factors. Anyone can learn kung-fu.

Because of the grace and ballet-like movement of the Northern style, women are especially attracted to its study. Children benefit from its emphasis on speed, discipline, and coordination.

The Northern style emphasizes low body movements and agile foot techniques as well as many hand combinations. Kicks, jumps, floor fighting, and speed footwork are excellent and essential for body conditioning. The Southern style relies more on hand techniques executed from a rather stationary position.

Kung-fu and karate share some fundamental movements, but they are two very distinct martial arts. True, karate developed from kung-fu. Still, no respectable karate instructor would claim to teach kung-fu, and no kung-fu instructor would claim to teach karate.

Kung-fu has no ranking belt system to categorize the various levels of proficiency. The student measures his advancement against others in his class and against more advanced students, who in turn measure themselves against the instructor.

There is no one prescribed uniform for kung-fu. For practice, the lightest and freest clothing is desirable. Shoes or kung-fu boots are often worn, but barefoot work for beginners is recommended.

A WORD ABOUT THE NORTHERN SHAOLIN SYSTEM

The Northern Shaolin System is the oldest system of kung-fu from Northern China, the center of the Chinese culture. The most widely practiced system in China today, it utilizes all conceivable ways of using one's hands, feet and body movement and, therefore, acts as a firm basis for learning other martial arts.

Because the Northern Shaolin System is known for its high kicks and swift footwork, it is often believed that hand techniques are not emphasized within it. This is not the case, for the hand techniques of the Northern System are as varied as the Southern System. All techniques of the Northern Shaolin System are executed with quick tension and short focusing time, a peculiarity that allows for fast, flowing movements and quick changes. And more than any other system, emphasis is placed on agility, general flexibility, stamina, speed and aesthetics. Classical form, too, is important to the Northern Shaolin System, arising from the belief that perfection of form will give greater coordination and a freer execution of techniques.

CONTENTS

LESSON 1

COURTESY
IN THE KWOON

THE SALUTE

Crouch slightly on your right leg with your right foot pointing 45 degrees to the outside. Your left foot is placed lightly about 10 inches in front of your right with the toes of your left foot pointing straight ahead and your left knee bent slightly. Most of your weight rests on your right foot. Your hands should be positioned in front of your chest with the knuckles of your right fist pressed into your left open palm.

The salute is performed upon entering or leaving the training area.

HORSE STANCE

Stand with your feet approximately three feet apart and your weight evenly distributed. Crouch with your hips forward as if you were sitting on a large horse.

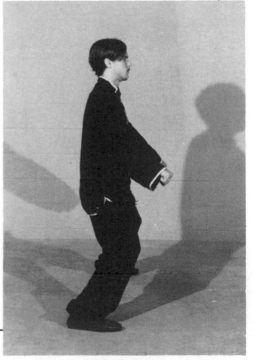

FRONT VIEW

SIDE VIEW

FRONT VIEW

FORWARD STANCE

Place your left foot in front of your right, two to three feet apart, and pivot the toes of both feet 45 degrees to the right. Keep your left knee bent, your right leg straight and the muscles of both legs poised, but relaxed enough for complete and instant control.

Reverse the leg positions for a right stance.

SIDE VIEW

FORWARD LEG LIFT

(1) Stand with your left leg in front of your right and lock your right knee. (2) Swing your right leg forward and upward while keeping your knee locked. Reverse the leg positions and repeat the exercise, working slowly toward your maximum height.

FRONT KICK

(1) Begin in a left forward stance. (2) Step forward, placing all your weight on your left leg and raise your right knee as high as possible with your right foot tucked back. (3) Extend your right leg while straightening your instep and bending the toes of your right foot backwards. (4) Snap your leg back into the cocked position. (5) Set your right leg back into your original left forward stance.

The entire kick should eventually become a single motion and relaxed control is essential. These points are important with all kicks.

FOOT BLOCKS

Foot blocks may be used defensively to block an opponent's attack or offensively to strike the opponent with the side of your foot.

INSIDE FOOT BLOCK

(1) Begin in a left forward stance. (2&3) Keeping your right knee straight, circle your right foot in front of and across your body by

lifting it out to your right, over your head and down on your left. (4) Set your right foot back into your original left forward stance.

A

B

OUTSIDE FOOT BLOCK

Outside foot blocks are executed by circling your foot in the opposite direction so that, for instance, your right foot would travel upward and

C

across your body first, then from the overhead position it would move outward to your right and down to the starting position.

D

PELVIC
ARCH STRETCH

(1) Place both feet flat on the floor about three feet apart with your left knee locked straight and your right knee bent. (2&3) Squat on your right leg so

that your extended left leg is as close to the floor as possible. (4&5) Repeat on the opposite side by extending your right leg and squatting on your left. Alternate from side to side.

LESSON 2

FRONT VIEW

HEEL STANCE

Place your right foot about 10 inches in front of your left with your heels in line and the toes of your left foot turned 45 degrees to the outside. The toes of your right foot face forward and are raised off the ground so your weight rests on your left foot and the heel of your right foot. Keep your left leg bent and your right knee flexed slightly.

A variation of this is the toe stance where the ball or toe of your right foot would rest on the floor instead of your heel. Your right knee should be bent more in the toe stance than in the heel stance.

SIDE VIEW

CROSS STANCE

From a natural standing position, cross your right foot behind and about 10 inches to the left of your left foot with the toes of your right foot facing the outside of your left and your right heel raised off the ground.

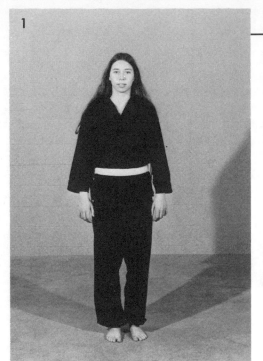

SIDE LEG LIFT

(1) Stand naturally with your feet together. (2) Lift your left leg out to the side and up with your knee locked. Your left hand will be positioned behind your leg when it rises and your right hand will be in front. (3) Drop your leg to its original position. Repeat with your other leg.

Relax and work slowly toward your maximum height.

NOTE: As an addition to the solitary exercise you can get a partner to lift your leg slowly to the side. Keep your knees locked and your instep bent.

SIDE
LEG SPLIT

(1) Stand with your feet parallel and spread to the sides as much as possible. (2-3) Place your hands just in front of you and on the floor to support your weight while leaning forward slightly and lowering

3

your body to the floor as far as possible. (4) When you reach your lowest position, arch your back.

Take special care not to force this exercise. Relax and go slowly.

4

SIDE KICK

(1) Begin in a horse stance. (2) With your right foot, step in front of and to the left of your left foot into a cross stance. (3) Balancing all of your weight on your right leg, draw your left knee up as high as possible and point it toward the direction of your kick while keeping your foot tucked back. (4) Extend your left leg so that the side of your foot lies on a line parallel to the floor. (5) Snap your left leg back into the cocked position. (6) Set your left foot down into a horse stance again.

HEEL STANCE, CROSS LEG AND SIDE KICK COMBINATION

(1) Begin in a left heel stance with your right arm extended low behind you and your left forearm held vertically about one foot in front of your face with your left fist closed. (2&3) As you shift your weight onto your left foot, draw your left fist to your chest and scoop your right open palm low in front of you and up along your left side. (4&5) As your right foot steps behind your left into a cross stance, execute a left punch in the direction you have just stepped while positioning your right open hand so that your thumb touches your left shoulder. (6-8) Keeping your hands in the same position, execute a left side kick. Retract your kick into whatever stance you find suitable for blocking.

This combination should be executed in a constant, flowing movement.

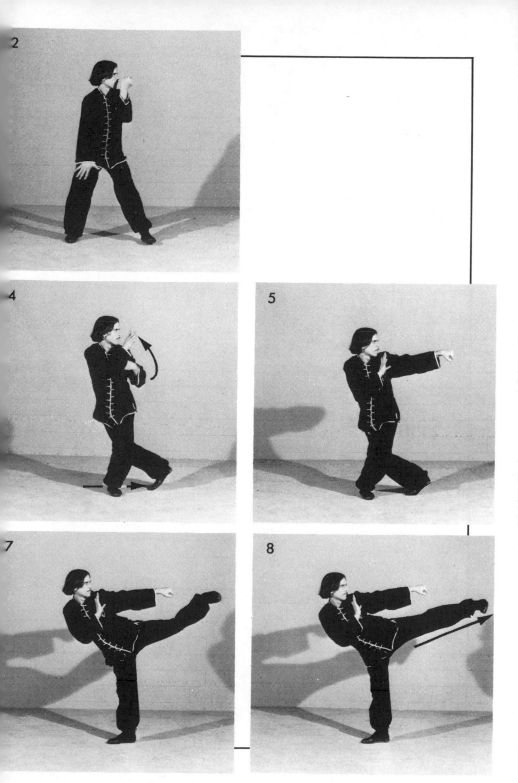

DEFENSE AGAINST SIDE KICK

(1) Stand with your left foot forward and raise your left arm as your opponent begins a right side kick. (2&3) Lean back on your right leg and deflect the kick with a left lower circular block. (4) Bend your left arm and lift up to trap your oppo-

nent's leg in the crook of your arm as you begin to step forward. (5&6) While holding the leg up, swing your right leg behind your opponent's supporting leg and push the opponent's face to your left to effect a trip over your leg.

LESSON 3

ROUNDHOUSE KICK

(1) Begin in a right forward stance. (2) Step up and balance on your right leg while bringing your left knee up high to the side and allowing your left foot to trail to the rear. (3) Pivot 45 degrees clockwise and extend your left leg in a horizontal motion. (Note: The kick pictured is angled upward for height.) (4) Retract your kick along the same path to the cocked position. (5) Set your left foot back into a right forward stance.

EXERCISES TO DEVELOP A BETTER ROUNDHOUSE KICK

SIDE KNEE LIFT

(1) From a standing position, keep one leg straight and bend the other at the knee. (2) Lift your bent knee as high as possible and hold that position. (3) Lower your knee to its

original position. Repeat several times with both legs.

This exercise is primarily designed to develop the muscles used in a round-house kick.

FRONT AND SIDE HURDLER'S STRETCH

(1) Sit on the floor with your right leg extended in front of you and your left leg bent and turned outward to the side. (2&3) Reach out with both hands and grasp your right foot, then pull your body forward as far as

4

5

possible without bending your right knee. (4-6) Recline until your back touches the floor. Repeat several times with both legs.

This exercise will give you flexibility for both the front kick and roundhouse kick.

6

STRAIGHT BACK KICK

(1) Begin in a right forward stance. (2) Step forward and cock your left knee up in front of you. (3) Extend your left leg directly to the rear with your heel

turned upward while watching over your left shoulder. (4) Snap your leg back into a cocked position. (5) Set your left foot down behind you into a right forward stance again.

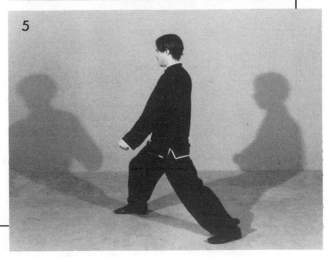

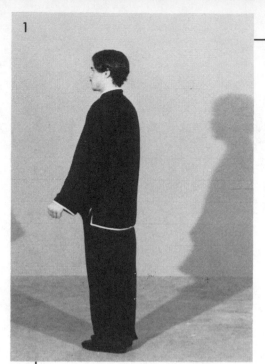
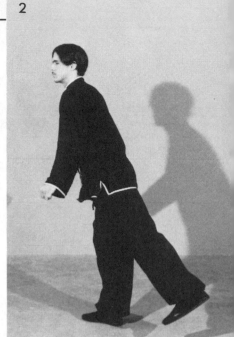

EXERCISE TO DEVELOP A BETTER BACK KICK

BACKWARD LEG LIFT

(1) Stand naturally with your feet together. (2-4) Swing your left leg back and up while keeping your knees locked. Repeat the exercise on both legs, working slowly toward your maximum height.

This stretch will help you develop your back kick.

NOTE: As an addition to the solitary exercise you can get a partner to lift your leg slowly to the rear and upward. Keep your form.

4

FOOT BLOCK SIDE KICK COMBINATION

This is a practical application of the foot block of lesson one and the side kick of lesson two.

(1) Begin in a right forward stance to your opponent's left stance. (2) As your opponent attempts to deliver a right front kick, deflect it with a left inside foot

block. Allow the retraction of your foot block to pivot your body 45 degrees clockwise. (3&4) When your opponent drops forward on his right leg, deliver a left side kick to his face. (5) Quickly retract your leg. (6) Thrust a second side kick into your opponent's midsection.

LESSON 4

CIRCULAR BLOCKS

When properly developed, variations of the circular blocks that follow will enable anyone to block any technique, regardless of the skill of the attacker. The defender utilizing the block has the advantage because the blocking arm travels a shorter distance than the attacker's offensive technique.

It is best to execute the block softly so it will be easier to change its direction or path when the situation demands. It is essential to practice until one can readily change the size of the circle entailed in the blocking maneuver. The hand may be open or close-fisted for the circular blocking exercise.

The designations "upper" and "lower" circular blocks describe the direction an attack would be deflected. Either block may be executed in a clockwise or counterclockwise motion.

A variation that will appear in later lessons is the "inward" circular block. Here the term designates the direction the block is thrown. An inward circular block, therefore, blocks *across* the body.

UPPER CIRCULAR BLOCKS

(1) Begin in a front stance with your left hand held open and palm down at waist level in front of you. Your fingers point to your right (2-4) Keeping your fingers pointed to your right, turn your palm forward and arc your hand up along the right side of your body and over your head. Lead the movement with the heel of your hand. (5&6) Arc your hand downward, closing it into a fist, palm up, and draw it to your hip.

VARIATION

The same motion may be used with your wrist held straight and your palm facing you. In either variation the forearm is primarily the point of contact.

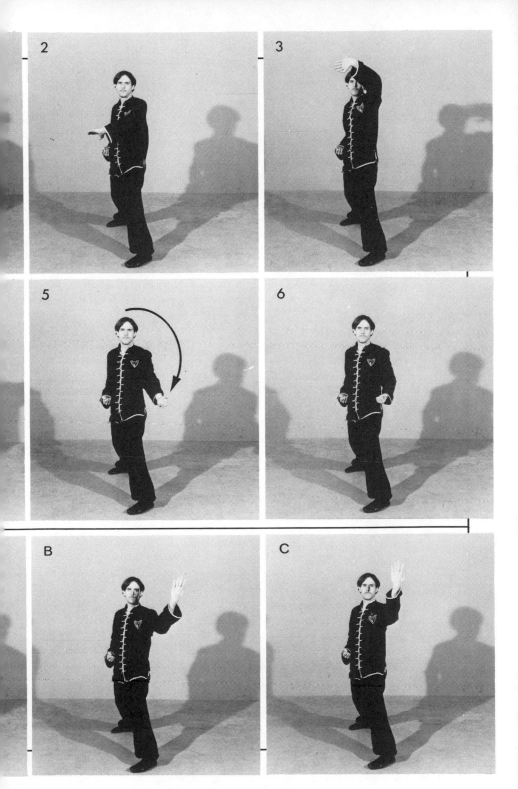

LOWER
CIRCULAR BLOCK

(1) Begin in a front stance with your left hand held open and palm toward you, just to the right side of your head. (2&3) Arc your hand down-

ward to full arm extension in front of and across your body to your left. During this movement keep your palm facing toward you.

APPLICATION

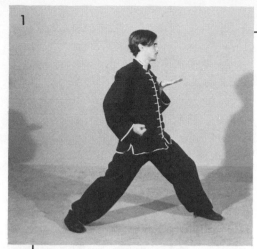

OPEN HAND TECHNIQUES

In kung-fu, open hands are used as well as the fists to strike. Open hand techniques are considered more advanced than the closed hand (fist). It takes longer to become proficient in open hand techniques, but once you become proficient with them, you'll find them more versatile, simpler and quicker to apply.

STRAIGHT KNIFE HAND

(1) Begin in a forward stance with the heel of your left hand close to your chest, your open palm facing upward and your fingers pointing forward. (2&3) Twist your hand as it moves forward until your fingers point upward and your palm faces forward.

Execute the straight knife hand with the same impact as a punch, the difference being in the contact method. In the straight knife hand, contact is made with the edge or the palm of your hand, whereas in the punch it is delivered with the knuckles.

During the movement, keep your body perpendicular and your shoulders straight and pressed down. The straight knife hand can also be executed from the hip and may be used as either a strike or a block.

SIDE KNIFE HAND

(1) Begin in a forward stance with your left hand extended palm down and behind your right ear. (2&3) Bring your hand straight forward, horizontally, by straightening your arm at the elbow, leading with the blade of your hand.

Tense your hand upon full extension of your arm or at the instant of contact and hit with the outer edge of your hand.

LOWER CIRCULAR HAND BLOCK AND STRAIGHT KNIFE HAND STRIKE

(1&2) When your opponent attempts to deliver a right knee attack, assume a left heel stance and deflect it downward and to the inside with a left lower circular block. (3) Your blocking hand continues its circular motion upward to guard your upper torso as well. (4) When your opponent attempts to follow through with a right punch, reverse your left hand's circular motion and deflect his

punch downward and to the outside with a second lower circular block. (5&6) At the same time, counter with a right straight knife hand, palm forward, to his face.

When deflecting your opponent's knee, make contact with your palm against either the inner or outer side of his knee where the force of his attack will not be as great as at the center or top of his knee.

LOWER CIRCULAR BLOCK AND SIDE KNIFE HAND STRIKE

(1) As your opponent attempts to deliver a right punch, assume a left heel stance and deflect it to your left and downward with the palm of your right hand. (2) At the same time, cock your left hand back to begin a side knife hand strike. (3) Shift your weight into a left forward stance as you deliver the side knife hand strike to your opponent's throat.

LOW PALM STRIKE

(1) Begin in a left forward stance. Your right open hand is at your waist, palm forward and fingers down. (2&3) Strike forward with the open palm by extending your right arm forward at a downward angle and turning your fingers to the outside.

In this strike as with all techniques the striking weapon and arm or leg that delivers it should tense at full extension. This tension should not be prolonged unnecessarily or the movement will become stiff and rigid. Simply tightening the muscles feels powerful but is not always useful power that can be transmitted to a target.

UPWARD PALM STRIKE

(1) Begin in a left forward stance with your hands in an open on-guard position. (2) Lower your right hand to your side, leaving your left hand up in a blocking position. (3&4) Strike forward in a rising arc with the palm of your right hand. Your fingers begin pointing toward the floor, but are kept straight and rise

with your arm. At the same time, your left hand sweeps downward across your body in a blocking motion that stops at the center of your chest.

This strike is most effective when striking low and in close, but contact may be made anytime during the upward arc.

LESSON 5

DOWNWARD KNIFE HAND STRIKE

(1) Begin in a left toe stance with your left hand open and extended in front of your face with the blade forward. Your right open hand is positioned just below your left elbow. (2) Lower your right hand to your side. (3) As you slide your left foot forward, lower your left hand in front of you, palm down, and circle your right hand back and up, behind your right ear with your palm facing outward. (4&5) Shift your weight forward into a left forward stance as you swing your left hand back and bring the blade of your right hand down in a chopping motion.

HORIZONTAL
BACKHAND STRIKE

(1) Begin in a forward stance with your left hand extended palm in and behind your right ear. (2&3) Bring

3

your hand straight forward, horizontally, by straightening your arm at the elbow, leading with the back of your hand.

APPLICATION

CIRCULAR
BACKHAND STRIKE

(1) Begin in a right toe stance with your right hand open and extended in front of your face with the blade forward. Your left open hand is positioned just below your right elbow. (2&3) Lift your left hand to face level as you lower your right hand with the palm facing you. (4&5) As your left hand lowers, palm down, draw your right hand up, between your left hand and your body and arc it forward into a right backhand strike.

2

4

5

COMBINATION FOR TWO-HAND FRONT GRAB

(1) As you stand naturally with your feet together, your opponent grabs your throat with both hands. (2) Using your forearms at 45-degree angles, step into a right forward stance and strike upward on the insides of your opponent's forearms to break his grasp. (3) Without stopping your motion, clap his ears with your palms while grabbing his head. (4&5) Pull his head down while lifting your right knee into his face. (6&7) As you drop your leg, thrust the arch of your foot down along his shin and to his instep.

HORIZONTAL
LUNGE PUNCH

(1) Begin in a standing position with your feet together. (2&3) As you step forward with your left foot, execute a right circular block that sweeps across your face and draw your left fist to your waist, palm up. (4&5) As your weight shifts into a left forward stance, execute a left punch, palm down, and stop your right circular block at the shoulder of your punching arm.

Be sure that the punch is in line with the direction your body is moving. Loss of alignment will result in loss of power from your body's momentum and you might as well be punching from a standstill. A lunge can also be applied to a vertical (fist) punch.

3

5

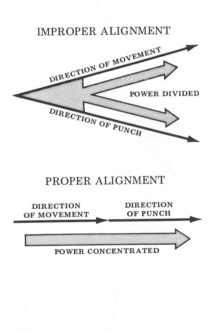

IMPROPER ALIGNMENT

DIRECTION OF MOVEMENT

POWER DIVIDED

DIRECTION OF PUNCH

PROPER ALIGNMENT

DIRECTION
OF MOVEMENT

DIRECTION
OF PUNCH

POWER CONCENTRATED

81

ROUNDHOUSE PUNCH

(1) Begin in a standing position with your feet together. (2) Step forward with your left foot and execute a right downward circular block across your face as you draw your left arm back. (3) As you shift your body

weight into a left forward stance, swing your left arm around and forward at face level with the first two knuckles of your left fist turned inward. (4) At the focus point of your punch, your right hand stops near your left shoulder.

POKE STANCE
AND LOW PUNCH

(1) Begin in a right forward stance. (2) Leap forward off your right foot while raising your left hand up and forward in a circular motion. (3) As you land on your left foot, keep your right hand tucked in and bring your left fist down in front of you. (4-6) Without stopping, slide your

right foot forward as you squat on your left leg and keep your left fist up by your right shoulder. Execute a right horizontal punch over your extended right leg.

The punch may be executed from the center of your body or from your right hip.

LESSON

UPWARD BACKFIST STRIKE WITH DOWNWARD PALM BLOCK

(1) In a front stance, extend your right arm, forehead level with your open palm facing downward, and drop your left fist back toward the rear. (2&3) Strike forward and upward with the back portion of the knuckles of your left fist while blocking downward to chest level with the palm of your right hand.

The downward palm block used here is the beginning of a lower circular block.

A

APPLICATION

In the application, as your opponent steps forward with his left foot and begins a strike with his right hand, step back with your left foot. Block his hand downward and to the outside with your right and deliver the upward backfist to his groin with your left.

B

C

D

SWINGING UPWARD PUNCH

A swinging upward punch is delivered in a motion similar to the upward backfist strike. The point of contact, however, is the front of the fist and the strike is thrown upward with a bent arm.

DOWNWARD HAMMERFIST STRIKE

(1) In a front stance, cock your right arm horizontally in front of your face with your palm open and facing outward. At the same time, cock your left arm behind you so that the palm of your fist faces the back of your head. (2&3) As you lower your right hand, blade forward in front of your throat, strike forward and downward with the bottom of your left fist.

APPLICATION

In the application, the hands are switched. As your opponent steps forward with his right foot and attempts to deliver a right punch, step forward with your left foot as you deflect it upward and to the outside with a left upper circular block. Then, step forward with your right foot to deliver the hammer strike with your right hand to his head.

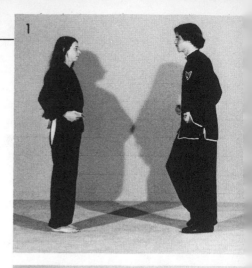

HAMMERFIST
KNIFE
HAND COMBINATION

(1) Stand naturally with your feet together. (2&3) As your opponent attempts to deliver a right punch, step back into a right forward stance and execute the beginning of a lower circular block, using your left forearm to deflect his blow to your right. At the same time, raise your right fist back behind your head. (4) Deliver a right hammerfist strike to your opponent's temple. (5-7) Step forward with your left foot and follow through with a left side knife hand strike to his throat.

5

CIRCULAR BACKWARD HAMMERFIST STRIKE

(1) In a right forward stance, look over your left shoulder and lift your left fist high as you guard with your right open hand. (2) Move your left arm downward, then up in a circular motion to hit with a hammerfist strike.

SIDEWAYS BACKFIST STRIKE

(1) Begin in a standing position with your feet together. (2) Step into a right forward stance and bring your left hand up in an inward circular block as you drop your right fist across your body. (3&4) As your blocking hand reaches your right shoulder, extend your right arm forward to strike with the back of your fist. Your arm is held horizontally.

Remember to tense your right arm and hand only at the point of full extension or contact.

LESSON 7

SPINNING REVERSE ROUNDHOUSE KICK

(1) Begin in a right forward stance.
(2) Shift all your weight to your right foot. (3&4) Begin a 360-degree spin by twisting your head and shoulders counterclockwise. (5-7) Keeping your left leg straight and looking over your left shoulder, use the momentum of your twist to lift your left leg up and around in a wide counterclockwise arc. (8) Immediately upon contact with your heel or at the focus of your kick, hook your left leg backwards at the knee.

The hooking motion at the end of the kick will add a final burst of speed to your kick and will redirect your momentum so that you can retract your leg straight back, assuming another right forward stance.

REVERSE ROUNDHOUSE KICK
(Executed without a spin)

(1) Begin in a horse stance. (2&3) Step behind and to the left of your left foot into a cross stance. (4&5) Shift your weight to your right foot, keep your left leg straight and swing it up and out in a wide arc. (6) Im-

4

5

mediately upon contact
with your heel or at the
focus of your kick,
hook your left leg back-
wards at the knee.

Upon completion of
the kick, step down
into another horse
stance.

6

FORWARD LEG SPLIT

(1) Bend your left leg at the knee and extend your right leg straight behind you. Arch your back while trying to keep your hips as low to the floor as possible. Ease up and down into this position several times by straightening and bending your left knee. (2) Extend your left leg forward, locking the knee, and lower your body to the floor as far as possible. Reverse the leg positions and repeat the exercise.

FRONT THRUST HEEL KICK

(1) Begin in a left forward stance. (2) Step forward, placing all your weight on your left leg and raise your right knee. (3) Extend your right leg while bending your toes and instep back as far as possible so that your heel is thrust forward. (4) Retract your foot by bending your leg at the knee before returning to your starting position.

As in the case of all kicks, the front thrust heel kick can be directed to targets of any height. Students who seek further advancement should develop the ability to kick high. Possessing this ability makes low kicks much easier and faster. For exercises to help develop high kicks, refer to earlier lessons and add the forward leg split covered in this lesson.

SINGLE LEG SQUAT

(1) Begin by standing on your right leg with your left leg extended in front of you. (2&3) Lower slowly to a full squatting position on your right leg while keeping your left leg straight and off the floor. (4) Slowly

straighten your right leg into your original standing position.

Do the exercise several times on one leg, then repeat it on the opposite leg. If you can't lower to a full squat, do the exercise with a half or quarter squat.

LESSON

ELBOW STRIKES

INWARD HORIZONTAL ELBOW STRIKE

This elbow strike should be thrown in a short arcing motion parallel to the floor. In the photos above where a left elbow strike is thrown from a horse stance, your shoulders and hips should rotate to the right with the strike.

FRONT UPWARD ELBOW STRIKE

The front upward elbow strike begins in a horse stance, but you shift into a forward stance as you deliver the blow. This gives the strike more power.

A

B

DOWNWARD ELBOW STRIKE

The downward elbow strike is thrown here in the horse stance. Raise your arm before the strike to give it power.

BACKWARD ELBOW STRIKE

This strike is thrown from a forward stance, which you reverse by looking back over your shoulder. Watch over the same shoulder as your striking arm. Power comes from your waist and forward leg.

DOUBLE FOOT SWEEP

(1) Begin in a left heel stance. (2) Turn 90 degrees counterclockwise and squat low on your left leg. Put your hands on the floor in front of you and extend your right leg out behind you. (3) Slide your right foot along the floor in a wide counterclockwise arc. (4&5) Shift your weight so that you squat on your right leg and extend your left. (6&7) Slide your left foot heel first along the floor in a wide 360-degree counterclockwise circle. (8) Upon completion of the double sweep, shift your weight evenly on both feet and rise into a horse stance.

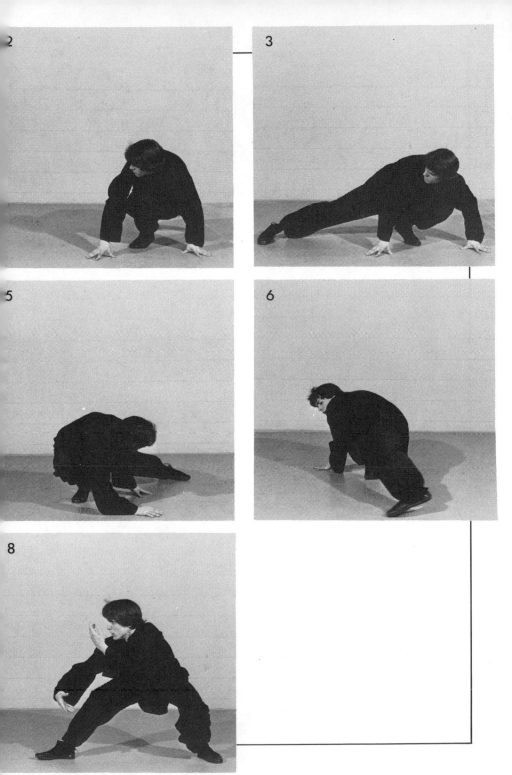

APPLICATION OF SWEEP

In the application, the double foot sweep begins as your opponent steps forward with his right foot and attempts to deliver a right punch. (A-E) You duck the right punch and force him to evade your first foot sweep by lifting his right leg. (F-H) Your second foot sweep catches his supporting leg.

HAND DEFENSE AGAINST REAR CHOKE

(1) While standing in a natural position, you are grabbed around the throat by an opponent behind you. (2-4) While lifting your right arm and knee, pivot clockwise toward him on your left foot. (5) Drop your right arm quickly to shake loose of his

hands. (6) Assume a right forward stance as you punch with both hands or deliver a lower hand strike to his mid-section.

Lifting your knee as you pivot helps you turn and may also be used as a knee strike.

HAND DEFENSE WITH FOOT SWEEP

(1) Face your opponent in a natural stance as he steps forward with his right and begins a right punch. (2) Step back with your left foot and deflect the punch with a right inward circular block. (3) Grab his arm with your blocking hand, position your left open hand across your

face and extend your left leg out low to your left. (4 & 5) While holding on to his arm with your right hand, deliver a left side knife hand strike to his throat and sweep to your right with your left leg so the arch of your foot strikes the back of his forward leg.

LESSON 9

KICKING COMBINATIONS

ROUNDHOUSE AND REVERSE ROUNDHOUSE KICKING COMBINATION

(1) Begin in a left forward stance. (2&3) Step forward and execute a high right roundhouse kick. (4&5) Retract your kick and set your foot down while shifting your weight off your left foot and turning your right heel toward the direction you just kicked. (6&7) Turning your head over your left shoulder first, rotate your body in a counterclockwise direction while executing a high reverse roundhouse kick. Be sure your kick hooks at the end by bending your left knee and retracting your foot straight back.

INSTEP
AND SIDE
KICK
COMBINATION

(1) Begin in a left forward stance. (2&3) Shift all your weight onto your left foot and thrust your right foot forward with your toes pointed to your right so that you strike with the arch of your foot. (4) While your right leg is still off the floor, propel your body up-

3

4

ward and forward,
drawing your left leg up
in a cocked position.
(5) Time your left side
kick so that it reaches
its full extension exact-
ly as your right foot
hits the floor. This
simultaneous reaction
will allow you to apply
maximum power to the
kick.

5

FRONT, ROUND, BACK KICK COMBINATION

(1) Begin in a left forward stance. (2&3) Execute a right front thrust heel kick. (4) Retract your kick to the cocked position. (5) Step down in front with your right foot while twisting your shoulders slightly clockwise. (6&7) Execute a left roundhouse kick while giving your hips an extra clockwise twist. (8) Retract your kick. (9) Set your left foot down just in front of your right. (10&11) Look over your right shoulder as you execute a right back kick.

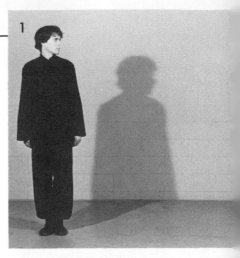

PUNCH, KICK COMBINATION

(1) Begin in a natural stance with your feet together. (2&3) Pivot 90 degrees counterclockwise and step out into a left forward stance. (4) Pivot 90 degrees clockwise into a horse stance as you execute a left punch to what is now your left side. (5) Pivot 90 degrees counterclockwise and execute a right straight punch. (6) Shift all your weight to your left foot. (7&8) Execute a left punch as you simultaneously execute a right front kick. (9&10) Set your right foot down in front of you and pivot 90 degrees counterclockwise into a horse stance as you execute a right punch to what is now your right side.

WRIST STRIKES

The wrist is also used as an effective striking surface in kung-fu. Make certain when the wrist is used for striking that you are not making contact with the back of your hand. All five fingers should be firmly held together with the wrist bent as shown in the following ready position. Well-timed focus tension is important.

INWARD WRIST STRIKE

(1) Begin in the ready position with your right hand in front. (2) Extend your left arm out and back with the back of your left wrist facing forward and your hand bent inward. (3) With your elbow very slightly bent, swing your left arm forward in an arc, leading with the back of your wrist.

APPLICATION

130

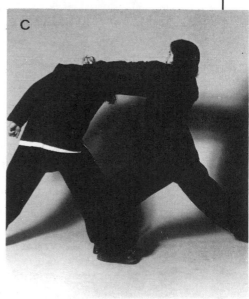

STRAIGHT WRIST STRIKE

(1) Begin with both fists held at your waist. (2) Raise your right hand, palm forward, as you curl your left hand inward. (3&4) Move your right hand across your body to your left

shoulder to block as you extend your left arm forward to strike with your wrist. Make sure your hand and fingers are curled toward you during the strike.

LESSON 10

DEFENSE AGAINST A TWO-HAND FRONT GRAB

(1) Stand with your left foot slightly ahead of your right as your opponent steps forward with his right and attempts a grab from the front. (2) Circle your right elbow upward and across your face to block and grab the inside of his right wrist with your right hand. The fingers of your right hand should be facing down with your thumb on the top of his wrist. (3&4) Step back with your right foot, as you pivot slightly to your right and twist his arm downward while raising your left hand high. (5) While holding his wrist firmly, strike downward on his elbow with your left forearm. (6) Draw your left fist back to your right shoulder as you position your left foot behind his right. (7&8) Deliver a left side hammerfist to his throat, knocking him back over your foot. (9&10) While still holding on to his wrist, deliver a right roundhouse kick to his face.

DEFENSE AGAINST A
SINGLE-HAND FRONT GRAB

(1) Begin in a natural standing position as your opponent steps forward with his left foot and attempts to grab you with his left hand. (2) Step back with your left foot and grab his wrist at the end of a left upward circular block. (3) Pull his arm to your left and raise your right arm. (4) Twist his wrist down and pivot slightly to your left as you deliver a horizontal elbow strike to his head. (5) Continue your motion and push down on his elbow with your right hand while lifting his wrist with your left hand. (6&7) Drop on the back of his knee with your right knee to force him to the floor.

4

5

7

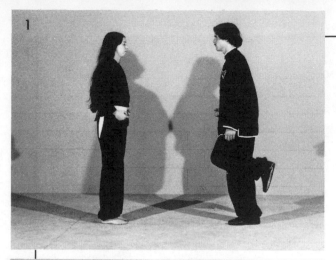

COMBINATION AGAINST A PUNCH

(1-3) From a standing position, block your opponent's right punch with a right upward circular block. (4&5) Use your blocking hand to grab your opponent's punching arm and pull him forward as you raise your right knee

and deliver a left straight knife hand to the side of his jaw. The knee can be used as a defense or an actual strike. (6) Complete the combination by stepping in a right forward stance and delivering a right punch to his chin.

ELBOW
AGAINST A GRAB

(1) Face your opponent in a standing position. (2-5) As he reaches out with both hands to grab

you, step forward with
your left foot and meet
him with a left upward
elbow to his chin.

CIRCULAR BLOCK AND PUNCH AGAINST A PUNCH

(1) Face your opponent in a standing position. (2&3) As he steps forward to attempt a right punch, step into a left forward stance and deflect his punch with a right lower circular block. (4&5) As your right arm blocks, pivot clockwise into a horse

3

stance and deliver a left punch to your opponent's ribs.

Your punch should connect just as you reach your horse stance to take advantage of the rotation of your body to add power to your strike.

4

5

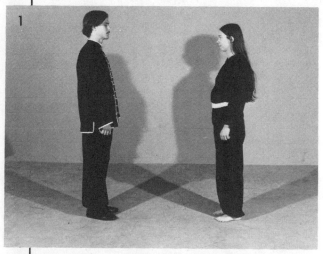

CIRCULAR BLOCK AND PUNCH AGAINST A KICK

(1) Face your opponent in a standing position. (2) As he begins a right front kick, step back with your left leg and raise your left hand in front of you. (3&4) When he kicks, deflect it to the outside with a

left lower circular block. (5) As he drops forward, pivot counter-clockwise into a horse stance and deliver a right punch to his mid-section, again using the rotation of your body for power.

LING-PO
(The continuous stepping form)

Kung-fu is a martial art of both defensive and offensive maneuvers. To perfect these techniques, you should practice them in a precise manner, according to the series of steps, the sum total of which comprises what is called a "form." The movements in each form should be natural and dancelike without any artificial stiffness or straining.

The form which follows is entitled *Ling-Po*, or "the continuous stepping." It is a basic form in the Northern Shaolin school required of a student before his first two months of training have ended. In practicing this form, one should first strive for precision before concentrating on artistic expression.

(1) Stand erect while facing straight ahead with your legs together and your hands at your sides. (2 & 3) Raise your hands palm forward until they are even with your ears, inhaling as you go. (4) Lower your hands palm downward until they are even with your waist, exhaling as you go. (5 & 6) Turn your right palm inward while you raise your left hand in front of you so that it is even with your chest. Your left palm should be pointed downward with your fingers

7

pointing across your chest. (7) Turn the palm of your right hand upward with its fingers pointed across your mid-section. You have now assumed the ready position. (8 & 9) Bend your right knee upward, lifting your right foot off the floor and then stomp it back to the floor while you step out into a left heel stance. (10 & 11) Execute a right open hand mid-block while simultaneously cocking your left arm for a left hand strike. (12-14) Execute a left open hand

10

strike while simultaneously stepping into a left forward stance. (15 & 16) Move your right foot forward so that you achieve a right toe stance while raising your right fist forward until it is level with your forehead and lowering your left fist to a point just in front of your hip. (17 & 18) Execute a right upward knee strike while simultaneously making a left open hand strike. Be sure to retract

your right fist to your hip. (19-21) Step down into a long right forward stance and execute a right fist punch while you maintain your left open hand block. (22-24) Maintaining your right forward stance, move your left open hand to your right armpit and execute a right hand side fist

21

25

strike in a circular motion. (25-27)
Step your rear foot ahead into a left
forward stance while simultaneously
executing a left open hand strike. Be
sure to retract your right fist to your
hip. (28 & 29) Maintaining your left
forward stance, execute a left up-

28

26

27

29

30

31

ward elbow strike. (30 & 31) Maintaining your left upward elbow strike posture, step your rear leg forward into a right forward stance and execute a right fist punch. (32-35) Step ahead with your rear foot into a right heel stance and execute a left open hand down block while retracting your right fist to your hip. (36) Slide your rear foot back so that you achieve a left forward stance and execute a high left open hand block.

34

32

33

35

36

37

(37 & 38) Execute a left open hand down block beneath your right armpit from the same stance while you make a right open hand strike at face level. (39 & 40) Twist your hips 90 degrees clockwise so that you achieve a horse stance and execute a left open hand strike while retracting your right fist to your hip. (41 & 42) Draw your left foot in toward your right and cock your left arm for an

40

43

open hand block. (43) Execute a left open hand block at medium height while you step forward with your right foot. (44) Continue stepping forward with your right foot until you have achieved a right forward stance, at which time you should complete a right bottom fist strike to the head area. Be sure to protect your face with an inner left open hand block. (45-47) Lift your rear foot and bring it around in back of your right so that you achieve a horse stance. Be sure to extend both arms down with your open palms pointing downward. (48 & 49) Maintaining your horse stance, cock your

46

44

45

47

48

49

left hand across your chest and execute a left open hand low block while retracting your right fist to your hip. (50-52) Step your right foot ahead into a right forward stance while you execute open hand chop, being sure to make a left open hand down block beneath your right armpit as well. (53 & 54) Twist your forward foot so that you achieve a horse stance and execute a right inner fist strike at medium height while making a left high open hand

52

50

51

53

54

block over your head. (55 & 56) Twist your hips 90 degrees counter-clockwise and straighten your right leg so that you achieve a left forward stance, from which point you execute a left open hand low block. (57) Draw your left leg in toward your right and execute a left open hand low block while retracting your right fist to your hip. (58-62) Bend your left knee upward, swivel your hips slightly clockwise and than ex-

61

ecute a left outward crescent kick
while blocking with your left open
hand and cocking your right fist.
(63) Following the kick, bring your
left foot straight to the floor and
block down with your left open
hand. (64) Step your right foot
ahead into a right forward stance
while you execute a right bottom fist
strike and a left open hand block.
(65) Shift your weight back to your
left leg and raise your right knee with
your toes pointing downward. At the
same time, execute a left straight
knife hand strike. (66) Lower your
right foot into a right forward stance
and execute a right straight knife

64

67

hand. (67 - 69) Make a right hand shoulder grab while stepping forward with your left leg and execute a foot sweep, sweeping outward with your left leg and pulling downward with both hands until you are squatting on your right leg. (70 & 71) Return to a standing position by straightening your right leg and turn your hips counterclockwise so that you achieve a short left forward stance. Be sure to cock both arms to your right for a block and strike combination. (72) Move your rear foot ahead into a right forward stance while you execute a right bottom fist strike and a

70

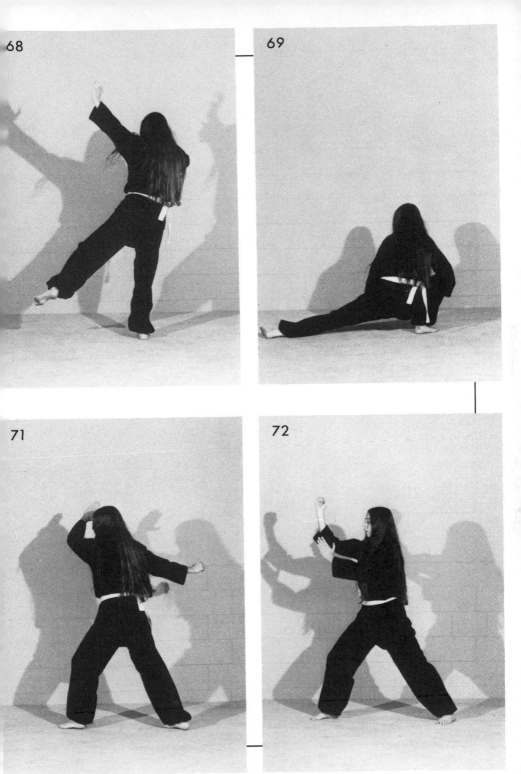

73

left open hand block. (73 & 74) Turn your upper torso 180 degrees counterclockwise and execute a left upward elbow strike. (75 & 76) Turn your upper torso back 180 degrees clockwise and execute a right upward elbow strike. (77 - 82) Grasp with

76

74

75

77

78

79

your right hand as you move your left foot 180 degrees clockwise and execute a foot throw. (83 - 87) Raise your right foot from the floor, turn

82

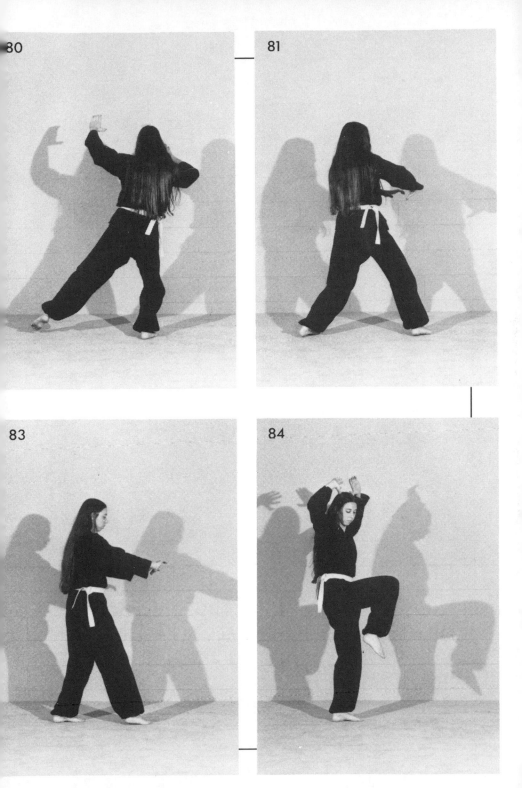

85

180 degrees clockwise on the ball of your left foot and execute a double palm strike to the groin in a right forward stance. (88 - 90) Turn your upper torso 180 degrees counter-clockwise on the balls of both feet into a left forward stance and simultaneously execute a left forearm block and a right lower palm block.

88

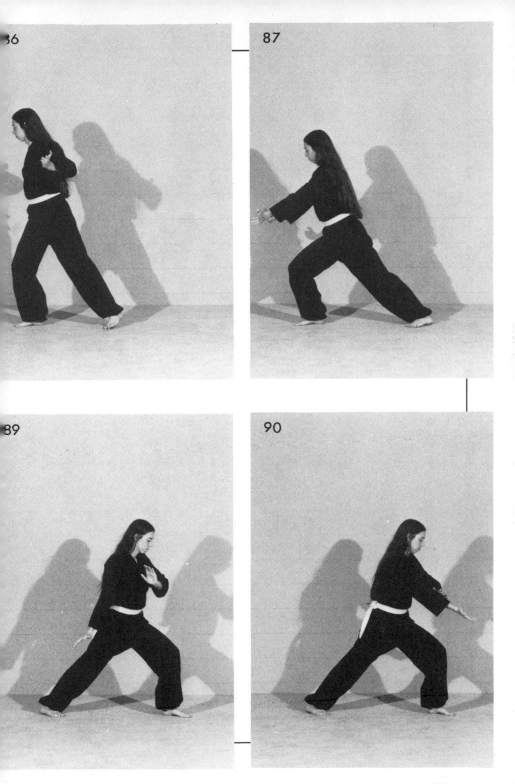

(91 - 93) Lean back into a left back stance as you grasp upward with your right fist and execute an upward left knee strike. (94 - 100) Step your right foot ahead into a right forward stance as you execute an arm lock technique, pushing your

97

left palm to the inside of your right elbow. (101 - 103) Step your right foot back so that you achieve a left heel stance and execute a left tiger

100

98

99

101

102

103

claw strike to the face. (104 & 105) Maintaining the same stance, grasp inward with your left hand. (106 & 107) Move your right foot ahead into a right heel stance while you simultaneously execute a right tiger claw strike to the face. (108 & 109) Step your right foot back so you achieve a left forward stance and execute a left

106

109

bottom fist strike. (110 - 112) Step back with your left foot so that you achieve a right forward stance and execute an arm lock technique with your left palm pushing in toward the inside of your right elbow. (113-116) Raise your right foot and pivot 180 degrees clockwise on the ball of your left foot. When the turn is com-

112

187

115

pleted, drop your right foot to the floor in a right forward stance and execute a double palm heel strike to the groin. (117-121) Lift your left foot up from the floor and pivot 180 degrees counterclockwise on the ball of your right foot. When the turn is completed, drop your left foot to the floor so that you achieve a left

118

116

117

119

120

forward stance and execute a double palm heel strike to the groin. (122-126) Slide your right foot forward into your left foot and perform the ceremonial hand movements to close the form.